May you always
have joy!
Love
Daphne

Daphne the Blind Dog

By Dawn M. Gibbons

Illustrations by Chad Thompson

With love and gratitude to my cousin
Cheryl Bruce for sparking the idea to
share Daphne's story, for the support
and encouragement along the way,
and for the many hours spent editing
with me over the phone.

Daphne was scared. She didn't know where she was. Everything was new and strange.

Daphne was a little, blind dog. She couldn't see anything, but she had other ways of understanding what was going on around her.

 Daphne could smell, so she knew there were lots of other animals around.

 She could hear a lot of *ruff, ruff,* and *meow* sounds.

 The wire walls of her kennel made Daphne feel safe and protected. Still, she was sad and lonely.

 Daphne longed so much for something better, but she didn't know what that was. In her heart, Daphne knew there was hope that things would change.

Daphne was taken out of her kennel and set down on a counter. She started to shake because she didn't know what was going to happen.

 She could smell that many other dogs had been on this surface.

 Daphne heard a *snip, snip, snipping* sound.

 She felt small tugs at her tangled fur. Gradually, she could feel the aches on her skin go away. She felt lighter and more comfortable.

 In her heart, Daphne knew that the people here were helping her.

 After her grooming, Daphne was carried outside in her kennel. She heard some *thumping* noises, then a *rumbling* sound. She knew these sounds. Car doors and an engine meant that she was being taken somewhere different.

When she arrived, Daphne could smell other animals.

 She heard a gentle voice say, "It's okay Daphne. We're going to make sure you're healthy and that you don't have any more puppies."

 When Daphne woke up from a deep sleep, her tummy felt just a little bit sore. However, her mouth felt more comfortable than it had before. With her tongue, she could feel that all the pointy things that were hurting so much were gone.

 In her heart, Daphne knew that she was being taken care of.

 She heard another voice say, "Even though you are blind and toothless, I'm sure we can find you a loving home." Daphne didn't know what it meant to have a loving home, but the kind voice gave her comfort.

One day, Daphne was taken out of her kennel and set down in another room. She could smell that someone new was there.

 Daphne felt warm and safe in the woman's arms.

 In her heart, Daphne knew there was hope for something better.

After a short visit, the woman said, "Daphne, my name is Dawn. I'm adopting you and we're going to be best friends forever!"

 Soon she heard the familiar *thump* of a car door, then the *rumble* sound of an engine. Where was she going now?

Inside the car, Daphne could smell something to eat. She nibbled on the tasty treat on the seat in front of her.

 She felt something soft under her body and a gentle rubbing on her back.

 In her heart, Daphne knew that good things were starting to happen.

"Go to sleep on your new blanket," Dawn whispered.

 Daphne had a nice nap. She woke up as she was carried out of the car. She heard some *click, click* sounds then a slow *creeeaaak*. She knew that she was going into a new building.

Daphne was set gently onto the floor. There were no wire walls to protect her. This place seemed so big. She didn't know where to go or what to do. She felt very nervous.

 "It's okay, Daphne. You're home now," Dawn said.

 Daphne could smell that Dawn was the only person around and there were no other animals.

 She had been to strange places before, so in her heart, Daphne knew that she could figure things out and it would be okay.

 She heard some *clickety-click* sounds and *splishing, splashing* sounds that were familiar. Daphne was hungry and thirsty, so she carefully moved towards the sounds of food and water.

As she walked, she bumped into things. Daphne could feel changes under her feet. The surface was cushiony and soft, then it was smooth and hard.

 The water was refreshing. The food was tasty and soft. Daphne could chew it, even without teeth.

 In her heart, Daphne knew that Dawn was kind.

 Suddenly, there was a soft *jingle, jingle* sound that was new to Daphne. Curious, she walked slowly towards the sound, bumping into things along the way.

Daphne could feel Dawn touching her nose to something. The small, round object moved and made the *jingle, jingle* sound again. Dawn said, "Ring the bell to go outside, Daphne."

Suddenly, Daphne felt a light breeze. She could smell something familiar. Daphne followed the scent of grass and went outside to pee.

In her heart, Daphne knew she would have everything she needed here.

Later, back inside the house, Daphne heard a *pat, pat, pat* sound. She wondered what it could be. Dawn was leading her to something else.

Daphne could smell her own scent where Dawn was patting her hand. Suddenly, she remembered! It was the blanket from the car. Her very own blanket.

As she stepped onto it, she could feel that underneath the blanket was something even softer. Daphne had never felt this kind of softness before and it was very comfortable.

In her heart, Daphne knew she could curl up and go to sleep and she would wake up in this wonderful new place.

"Good night, Daphne. It's been a big day," Dawn said.

In the morning, Daphne heard that new *jingle, jingle* sound again and "It's time to go outside."

Daphne felt a harness get wrapped snugly around her body. When she felt a light breeze, she knew it meant she could go outside. She felt a gentle tug on the harness, so she took a step in that direction.

 As she stepped, she could smell something yummy. She took a few more steps and got a tasty reward.

 Distracted, Daphne stopped to listen. She heard *vroom, vroom* noises going by. She heard *tweet, tweet* sounds up in the trees. She heard a *snap, snap* sound and then, "Come on, Daphne. Walk to Dawn."

 She followed the tug on her harness, the smell of the treats, and the sound of Dawn's fingers snapping. She took a few more steps.

 In her heart, Daphne knew that she could do this!

One day Daphne heard the *splash, splash, splashing* sound of running water. "It's time for a bath," Dawn said.

 When the warm water flowed over her body, Daphne shook with fear. She felt Dawn rubbing her all over.

 There was a soft, sweet smell that tickled her nose.

 Because Dawn was there, in her heart, Daphne knew that whatever was happening was a good thing. She could begin to relax.

Every day, Daphne had fresh water and soft, tasty food. She grew to be a healthier size.

The smell of tasty treats helped
her learn her way around
without bumping into things.

Daphne knew how to ring the bell when she needed to go outside.

She liked riding in the car to explore new places. Dawn was always there to support her when she was nervous.

Over time, Daphne gained the confidence to lead the way when she walked a familiar path.

She got to sleep in her very own soft, comfy bed.

 All the smells of Daphne's new home became familiar.

 Every night before bed, she felt comfort in Dawn's arms and enjoyed a nice rubbing on her body.

 She would hear Dawn say, "I love you, Daphne."

 In her heart, Daphne knew she had found what she had longed for - joy!

 FriesenPress

Suite 300 - 990 Fort St
Victoria, BC, V8V 3K2
Canada

www.friesenpress.com

ISBN
978-1-5255-4916-8 (Hardcover)
978-1-5255-4917-5 (Paperback)
978-1-5255-4918-2 (eBook)

1. Juvenile Nonfiction, Animals, Dogs

Distributed to the trade by The Ingram Book Company